To: Autumn

NANPo '95

FROM: Nana + Poppa

# The Lord is my
# Shepherd

Bible Verses of
Comfort and Encouragement
for Children of All Ages

**Chariot Books**™
David C. Cook Publishing Co.

Chariot Books is an imprint of David C. Cook Publishing Co.
David C. Cook Publishing Co., Elgin, Illinois
David C. Cook Publishing Co., Weston, Ontario
Nova Distribution Ltd., Torquay, England

THE LORD IS MY SHEPHERD

Illustrations by Connie Bieber
Designed by Elizabeth Thompson and Dawn Lauck

First printing, 1991
Printed in the United States of America
95 94 93        5 4 3 2

Bible, English. New International. Selections. 1991
The Lord Is My Shepherd and other favorite Bible verses.
p. cm.
Summary: A collection of brief selections from the Bible to introduce the concept of
the protection offered by God.
ISBN 1-55513-680-X
[1. Bible—Selections.]  I. Chariot Books.  II. Title.
BS391.2 1991
220.5'208—dc20
91-17532
CIP
AC

*Dedicated to children everywhere
who, like their parents and
grandparents, will find comfort and
encouragement in these timeless
verses from God's Word.*

# The Shepherd's Psalm

The Lord is my shepherd,
   I shall not be in want.
     He makes me lie down in green pastures,
he leads me beside quiet waters,
     he restores my soul.
He guides me in paths of righteousness
     for his name's sake.
Even though I walk
     through the valley of the shadow of death,
I will fear no evil,
     for you are with me;
your rod and your staff,
     they comfort me.
You prepare a table before me
     in the presence of my enemies.
You anoint my head with oil;
     my cup overflows.
Surely goodness and love will follow me
     all the days of my life,
and I will dwell in the house of the Lord
     forever.

PSALM 23

# The Lord's Prayer

Our Father in heaven,
Hallowed be Your name.
Your kingdom come.
    Your will be done
On earth as it is in heaven.
    Give us this day our daily bread.
And forgive us our debts,
    As we forgive our debtors.
And do not lead us into temptation,
    But deliver us from the evil one.
For Yours is the kingdom and the
    power and the glory forever.
Amen.

MATTHEW 6:9-13 (NKJV)

# Don't Be Troubled

Peace I leave with you; my peace I give you. I do not give to you as the world gives. Do not let your hearts be troubled and do not be afraid.

JOHN 14:27

# Do Not Worry

Therefore I tell you, do not worry about your life, what you will eat or drink; or about your body, what you will wear. Is not life more important than food, and the body more important than clothes? Look at the birds of the air; they do not sow or reap or store away in barns, and yet your heavenly Father feeds them. Are you not much more valuable than they? Who of you by worrying can add a single hour to his life?

But seek first his kingdom and his righteousness, and all these things will be given to you as well.

MATTHEW 6:25-27, 33

# Jesus and the Children

People were bringing little children to Jesus to have him touch them, but the disciples rebuked them. When Jesus saw this, he was indignant. He said to them, "Let the little children come to me, and do not hinder them, for the kingdom of God belongs to such as these."

MARK 10:13, 14

# The Good Shepherd

I am the good shepherd. The good shepherd lays down his life for the sheep. The hired hand is not the shepherd who owns the sheep. So when he sees the wolf coming, he abandons the sheep and runs away. Then the wolf attacks the flock and scatters it. The man runs away because he is a hired hand and cares nothing for the sheep.

I am the good shepherd; I know my sheep and my sheep know me—just as the Father knows me and I know the Father—and I lay down my life for the sheep.

JOHN 10:11-15

# Many Rooms

D o not let your hearts be troubled. Trust in God; trust also in me. In my Father's house are many rooms; if it were not so, I would have told you. I am going there to prepare a place for you. And if I go and prepare a place for you, I will come back and take you to be with me that you also may be where I am.

JOHN 14:1-3

# Go, and Jesus Will Be With You

Go and make disciples of all nations, baptizing them in the name of the Father and of the Son and of the Holy Spirit, and teaching them to obey everything I have commanded you. And surely I am with you always, to the very end of the age.

MATTHEW 28:19, 20

# My Help Comes From the Lord

I lift up my eyes to the hills—
    where does my help come from?
My help comes from the Lord,
    the Maker of heaven and earth.

He will not let your foot slip—
    he who watches over you will not slumber;
indeed, he who watches over Israel
    will neither slumber nor sleep.

The Lord watches over you—
    the Lord is your shade at your right hand;
the sun will not harm you by day,
    nor the moon by night.

The Lord will keep you from all harm—
    he will watch over your life;
the Lord will watch over your coming and going
    both now and forevermore.

PSALM 121

# God Loves Us So Much

How great is the love the Father has lavished on us, that we should be called children of God! And that is what we are! The reason the world does not know us is that it did not know him. Dear friends, now we are children of God, and what we will be has not yet been made known. But we know that when he appears, we shall be like him, for we shall see him as he is.

I John 3:1, 2

# God Helps Us in Trouble

God is our refuge and strength,
an ever-present help in trouble.
Therefore we will not fear, though the
earth give way
and the mountains fall into the
heart of the sea,
though its waters roar and foam
and the mountains quake with their surging.

PSALM 46:1-3

# Because of Jesus, I Will Live Forever

Jesus said . . . "I am the resurrection and the life. He who believes in me will live, even though he dies, and whoever lives and believes in me will never die. Do you believe this?"

JOHN 11:25, 26

# Jesus Gives Me Strength

I can do all things through Christ who strengthens me.

PHILIPPIANS 4:13 (NKJV)

# God Always Helps
# Those Who Love Him

And we know that in all things God works for the good of those who love him, who have been called according to his purpose.

ROMANS 8:28

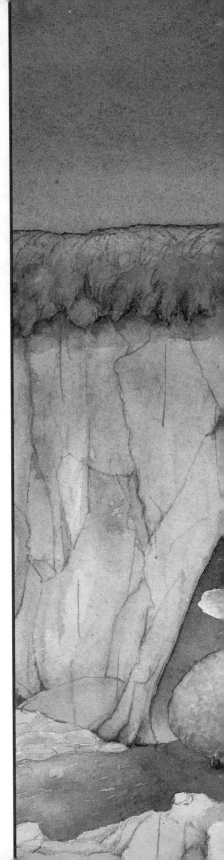

# God's Gift to You and Me

For God so loved the world that he gave his one
and only Son, that whoever believes in him
shall not perish but have eternal life.

JOHN 3:16